First published in Australia by Wild Eyed Press, 2018
Wild Eyed Press, 33 Warren Road, Nannup WA 6275
wildeyedpress.com.au

Text copyright © Kate Capewell 2018
Illustration copyright © Marion Duke 2018

Cover and layout design by Marion Duke

All rights reserved. No part of this publication may be reproduced, stored in a retrieval system, or transmitted in any form or by any means, electronic, mechanical, photocopying, recording or otherwise, without the written permission of the publisher.

Written, illustrated and designed in Australia
Printed in Australia

ISBN 978-0-6481611-4-1

Z

Zeds: You usually catch some zeds when you're Zonked out.
Zonk: When you "Zonk out" or have "Zonked it", you are exhausted and have gone to sleep.

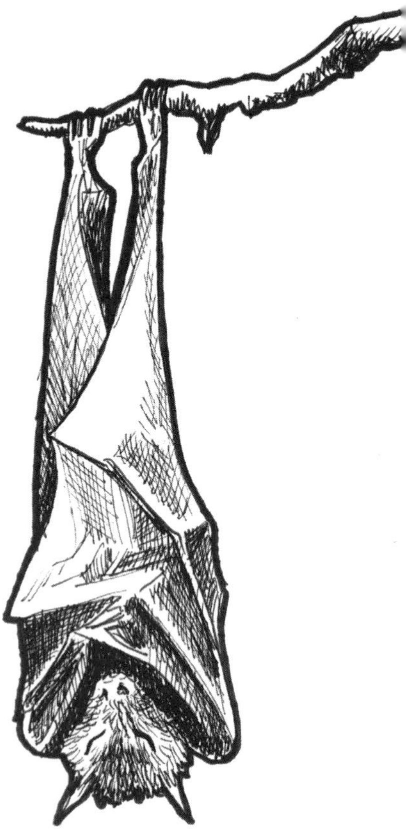

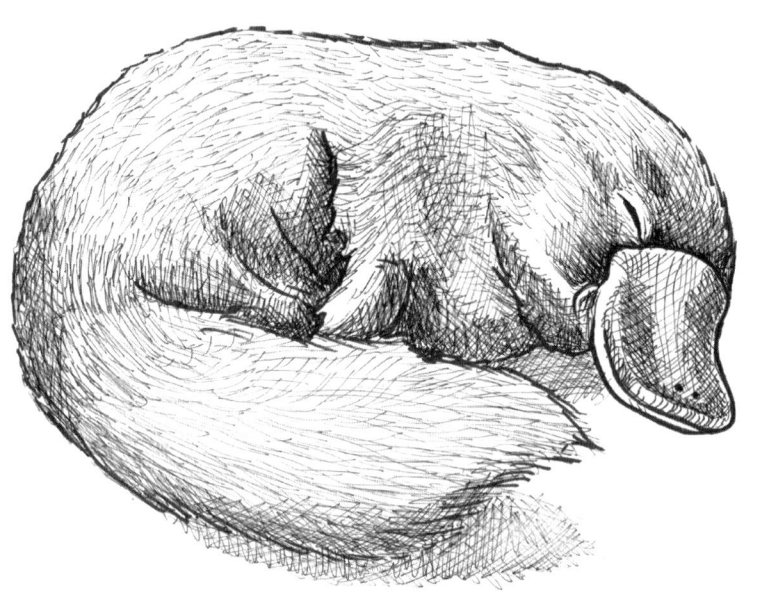

Yabby: Australian freshwater crustacean. Known by different names depending on which Australian state you are in.

Yakka: Normally preceded by the word "hard", yakka is referring to work.

Yarn: Having a chat, or telling a long and involved story.

Yeah nah: No.

Yonks: A long time.

You beaut: Used in a sentence when something is very nice, or very flashy.
"He was driving his you beaut sports car."

You bewdy (You beauty): Fantastic. Can also be extended to "*You bee-yew-tee*"

You're Un-Australian: Perhaps the biggest insult ever. The response to this is usually, "maaaaate."

Youse: A term referring to more than one 'you'.

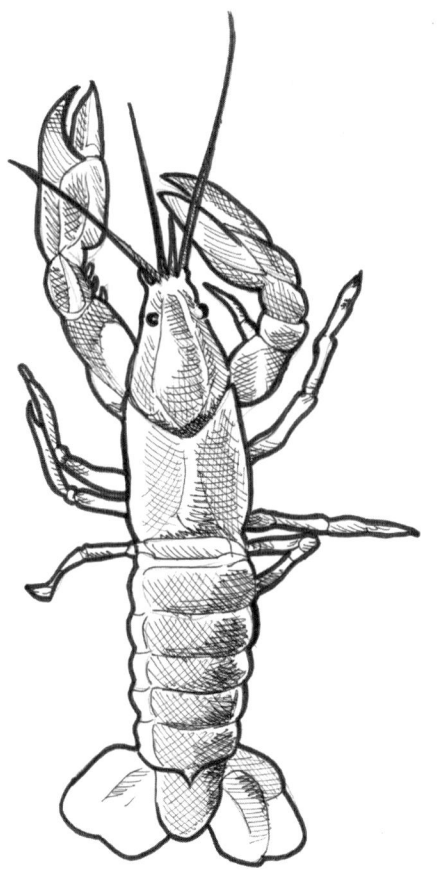

XXXX (four-ex)**:** Beer. Bitter, Gold or Summer Bright – Four-ex is brewed in Brissie, Queensland. It's also the only bloody thing we have starting with an X.

Woop-woop: A term for a place of no particular interest. Also, "Out Woop Woop", which means very far away.

Wuss *(wooss* pronounced with *oo* as in book or cook)**:** A coward; a frilly knickered, girly bloused, sooky la-la. Not considered offensive unless you're a wuss.

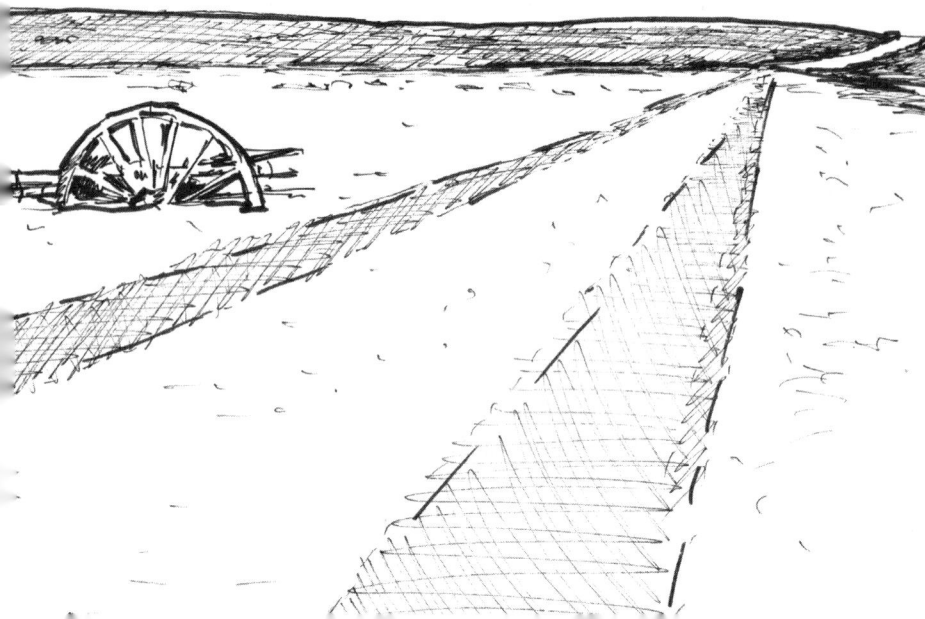

What do you reckon *(wod-da-ya-reckon)*: Said very quickly, so it actually sounds like one word. A question asked when someone would like your opinion.

Whinger *(win-jah)*: One who complains. To put whinger, wanker and pom in the same sentence is to invite a bout of fisticuffs with the person you are insulting, if they're British and understand what you're saying.

Wombat: an angry ground-dwelling marsupial.

Woobla: Wine.
"Would you like a flagon of woobla, mate?"
"Don't mind if I do."

W

Wag/Wagging: Playing truant.

Walkabout:
1) A solitary journey into the Bush to get away from it all and do a bit of contemplation of the navel.
2) Something or someone who is not where it/they are supposed to be.
"He went walkabout".

Wanker: A self-obsessed person.

Way out to billy-o: A long way away.

Westie: A person from Western Australia. Also called a sand groper.

Wetty: A wetsuit for diving or surfing.

Whack:
1) To put.
2) To hit.
Whack something on: to get dressed.

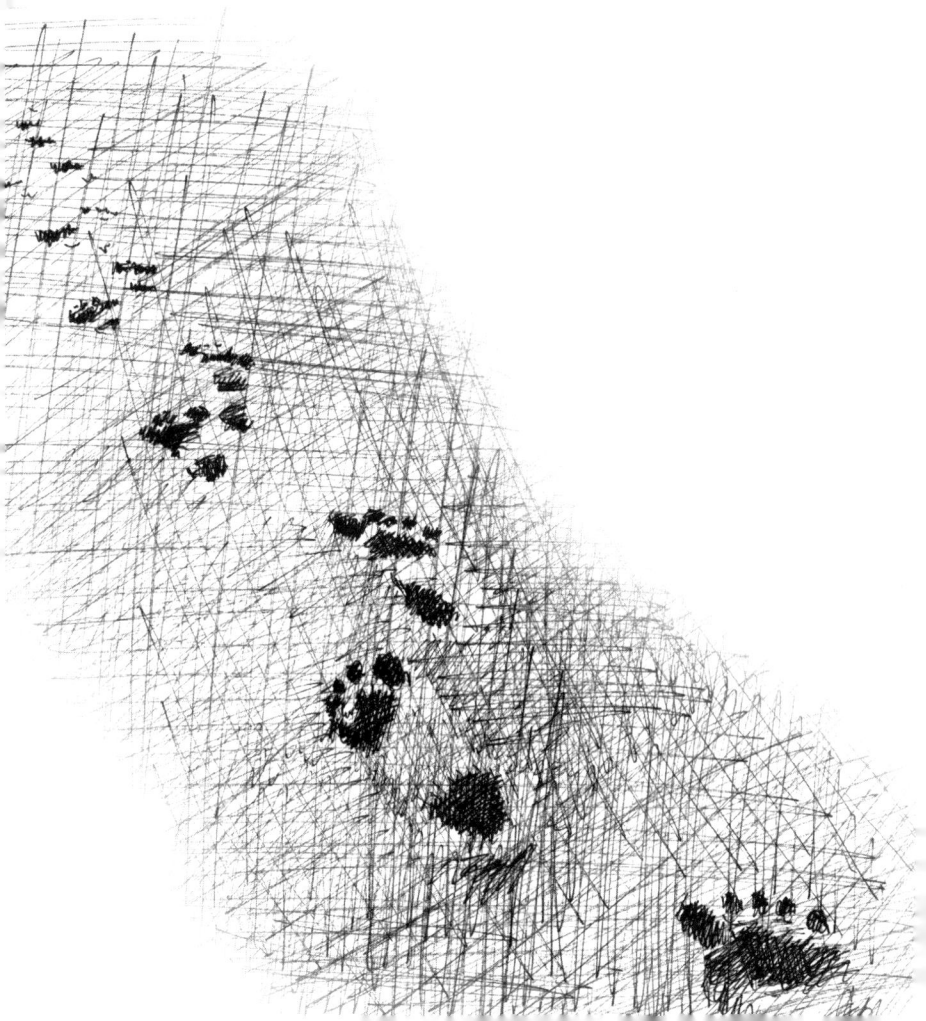

V

Vanilla Slice: A delectable treat consisting of firm vanilla custard sandwiched between two slices of thin pastry and topped with icing.

Veg out/Vegging out *(vej out/ vejjing out)*: To completely relax.

Up the duff: To be pregnant.
Up the road: See Down the Road.
Ute: Utility vehicle or pick-up. Unfortunately some car companies are slowly trying to phase out the word "Ute". The origin of ute goes back to a well-known story from 1932, where the unknown wife of a Victorian farmer wrote to Henry Ford asking for "a vehicle to go to church in on Sundays and which can carry our pigs to market on Mondays". Ford nicknamed the vehicle the "kangaroo chaser", a coupe utility which had a two-door cab on a passenger car sedan chassis with an open tray on the back. It has since evolved from being in only two-wheel drive to four-wheel drive models and is available from a number of different car companies. The ute is an Aussie icon and the name itself should not disappear into history.

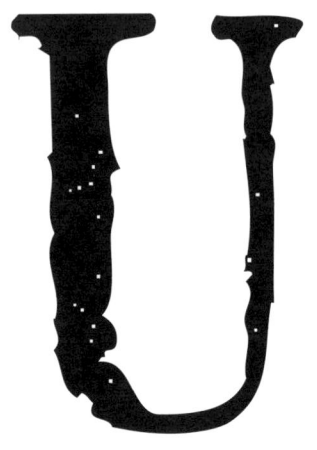

Uggies: Genuine wool-lined sheepskin boots. Uggies are often worn as slippers, though if you're feeling like a bit of a Bogan, you can wear them to the shops.

Un-Australian: When someone is not living up to the generosity and goodwill that is considered "Australian".

Up the creek: To be in trouble with no viable escape. Also known as, "up shit creek."

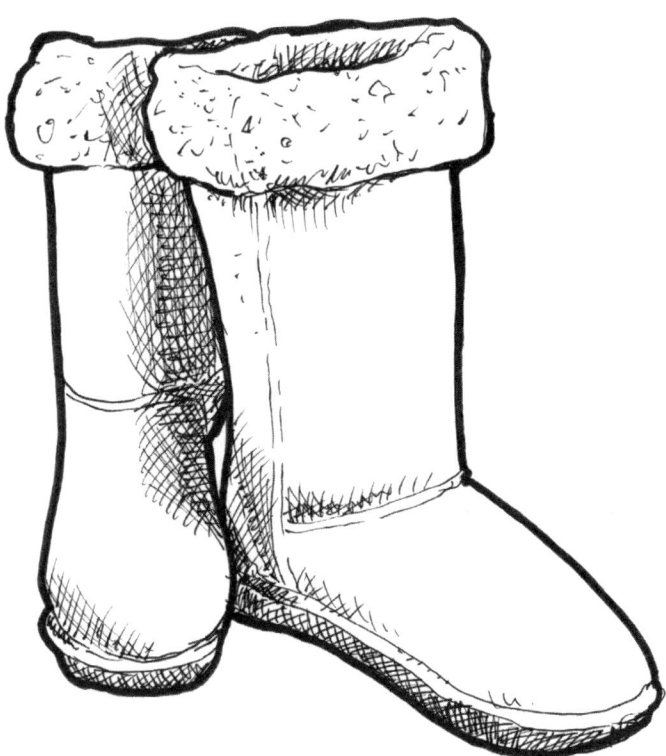

Troppo: "Going troppo" is to go insane. Originally from The top end, to "go troppo" is a side effect of long exposure to tropical heat, which can make people a little crazy. It has now come to all parts of Australia and refers to anyone who seems to have gone slightly nuts.

Two up: A betting game or game of luck played on Azac Day. Illegal to play any other day of the year. For more information on Two-up, it is best to go to a game.

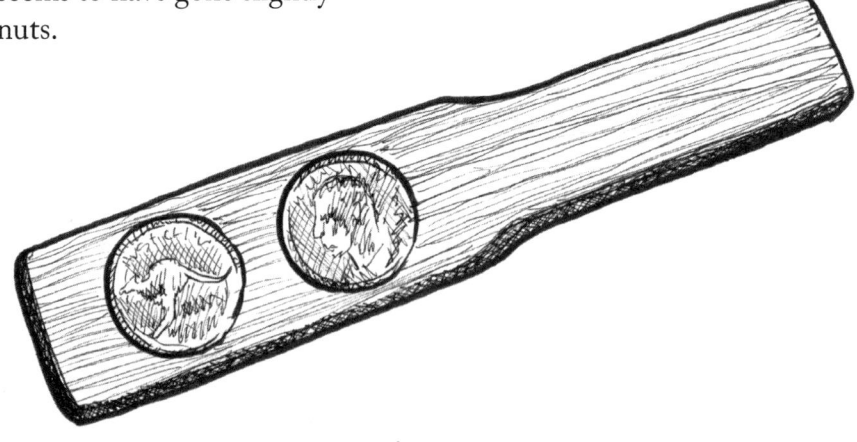

Tiger Snake *(or Tigery)*: A large, striped venomous snake that ranges in colour from olive green to black. Don't go near them.

Tinny:
1) A can of beer.
2) A small aluminium boat.

Toastie (British): A toasted Sandwich. Not to be confused with a toast sandwich, toasties are filled with ham, cheese, tomato. There are many delicious recipes for toasted sandwiches, and even more so with Jaffles.
Togs: See Swimmers.
Too right: "I agree wholeheartedly."
Trackies: Comfortable, casual wear. Also known as trackie dacks.
Tradie: A qualified tradesman. Trades include plumber, boilermaker, builder, brickie, chippie, roofer, sparky, and tiler.

Tassie tiger: Though there have been occasional 'sightings' of the Tassie tiger, the animal is believed to have been extinct since 1936, when the last known living specimen died in captivity.

Ta-ta *(tah-taarh)*: an expression of farewell.

Tea: Unless you're having a cuppa tea, it is referring to the evening meal. Also known as dinner.

'What's for tea?'
'I'm thinking of grabbing a cooked chook from the supermarket."

The Olds: Parents.

The top end: The northernmost part of Australia, in the Northern Territory.

Thongs: You wear them on your feet. You'll figure it out. Good luck.

resent those who have become 'out of touch' with regular Aussies as a result of their good fortune or social standing. Therefore, in this example, the consensus is the "Tall Poppy' should be "cut down to size".

One who suffers from Tall Poppy Syndrome is ridiculed and belittled.

Tassie: Tasmania, also known as "The Apple Isle."

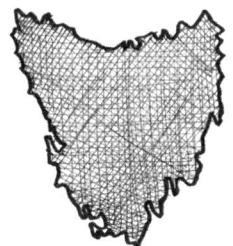

Tasmanian devil/ Tassie devil: A ground-dwelling marsupial of dubious character with large, sharp teeth.

Ta *(tarh):* An expression of thanks.

Taking the mickey: Origin Cockney. To tease mercilessly. See Piss, 4)Taking the piss.

Tall Poppy/Tall Poppy Syndrome: Is often referred to as begrudging of someone who is doing better than oneself. This is incorrect in Australia due to its unique cultural standing on the idea of Social Class; the belief that everyone is equal regardless of social background. Aussies do not begrudge those of their peers who are doing well in life; in fact, they commend them. Aussies do

Swifty: When someone is "pulling a swifty" they are trying to mislead you. Don't allow it.
"To pull a swifty" is also known as "to pull a fast one" "to pull the wool over one's eyes".

Swimmers: Garments worn for swimming. Also called Cossies, Togs or Bathers.

Squealie: To make the tyres of one's vehicle "squeal" by accelerating rapidly from a stationary position.

Stuffed:
1) "I'm Stuffed" means I am very tired.
2) "Can't be stuffed" means I neither have the inclination or energy to do this thing.
3) "Get stuffed" means I am requesting that you go and do something physically impossible to your own body for my personal enjoyment.
4) "It's stuffed" means it is broken.
5) "Stuffed up" means I made a mistake.

Swag: Originally a bedroll used by a 'Swagman' to sleep in, the swag is now like a mini-tent for one (or two) that consists of a mattress inside a canvas covering. Very handy for camping or when you're going bush.

Steak: Generally, refers to a tender cut of beef.

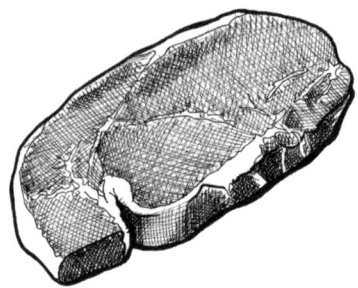

Sticky beak: A nosy person, or one that is overly curious. To 'have a sticky beak' is to have a look at something.

Stone the Crows: Accompanied by an exclamation mark, this old Aussie term is usually one of great surprise. Origin unknown.

Straya *(stray-ya)*: The best country in the world.
Strine: Australian English.
Struth: An exclamation of surprise or disbelief.
Stubbie/s:
1) 375mL brown glass bottle of beer.
2) A pair of work shorts.

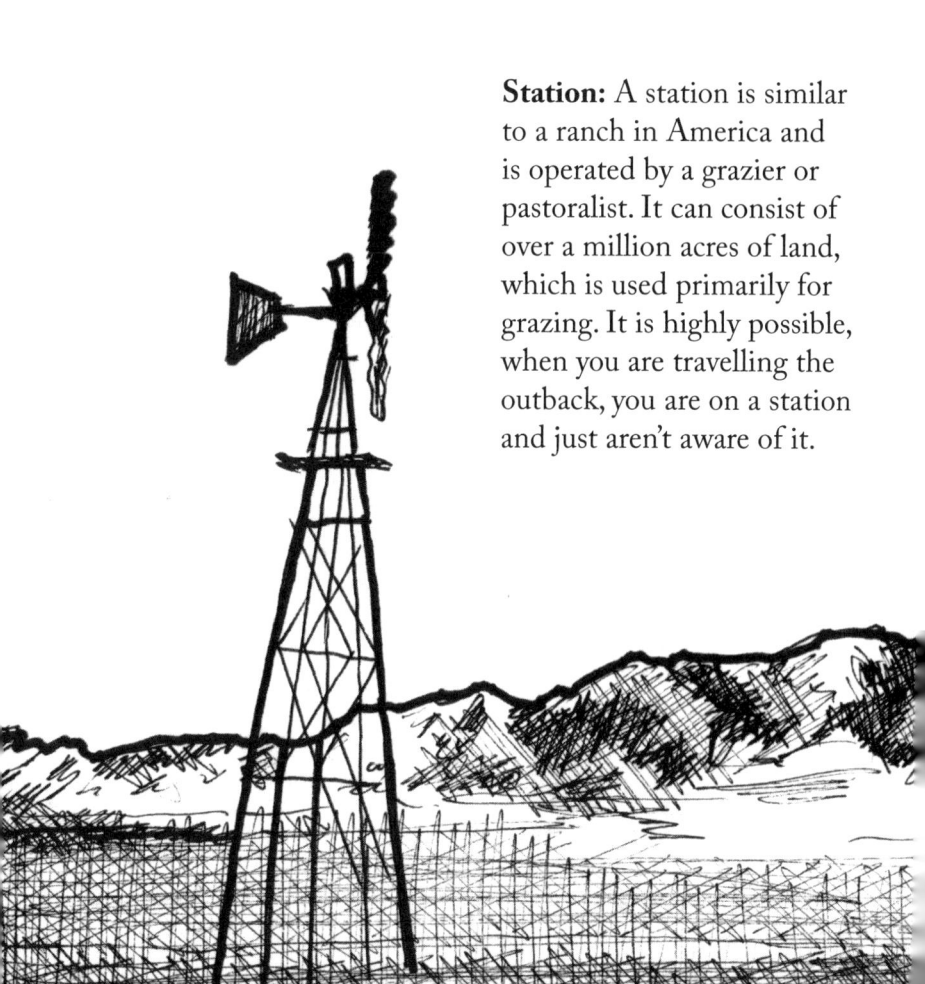

Station: A station is similar to a ranch in America and is operated by a grazier or pastoralist. It can consist of over a million acres of land, which is used primarily for grazing. It is highly possible, when you are travelling the outback, you are on a station and just aren't aware of it.

Smoko: A short break to have a cuppa, something to eat, a cool drink from the esky or a durry during working hours.

Snag/Snagger:
1) Sausage.
2) Sensitive New Age Guy.

Spaggie Bog/Spag bog/Spag Bol: Spaghetti Bolognese.

Sparky: A qualified electrician. See Tradie.

Specky: A shortened version of the word "spectacular".
"Did you see Oldmate fall off the back of the Ute?"
"Yep. It was pretty specky."

Speedo: Speedometer or odometer. If you are "checking your speedo", you're seeing how fast your vehicle is going. If someone asks for your "speedo reading", they want to know your odometer reading.

Speedos: Mens swimwear. Also called Budgie Smugglers.

Spider: Aside from the usual use for "spider", this is also a drink made with Cool Drink and ice-cream.

Squizz/squizzy: To look.

Sick *(sic)*:
1) Very cool, 'Sick as'. When something is "fully sick" it is better than very cool.
2) To do something. When someone "cuts sick", "goes sick" or "went sick", they possibly are doing/did burnouts in their hotted-up hoon wagon (car), or they went a little crazy.

Skitz/skitzo: To be upset and angry. "He was going skitzo" means he was very upset and throwing things around. "I'm gonna skitz out on that bloke." Means I am going to show that gentleman exactly how upset I truly am.

Slab: A term for a cardboard box containing 30 cans of beer.

Slacker: A lazy person. Also known as a "slack arse."

Slash: When someone is "having a slash", they are urinating.

Slip, slop, slap: To protect oneself from getting sunburnt. Literally, slip on a shirt, slop on sunscreen and slap on a hat. It is very good advice in the harsh Australian summer. Heed it well.

Shoot through: to leave. Therefore, when one says, 'he shot through', it means, 'he left'.

Shout: When someone "shouts you" a drink or a meal, it means they are buying it for you. If it's "your shout", it's your turn to buy the drink or meal. If you say, "It's my shout", you are offering to buy for whomever is with you. If you are, "shouting the bar", you are buying everyone in the pub a drink. Originally, people took turns to shout a round of drinks, where each round was bought by a different person in the group. Occasionally someone would go missing when it was their shout. It was very Un-Australian.

Sheep shagger: A New Zealander. Also called a Kiwi.
Sheila: An old-fashioned term for a female.
She'll be right: Everything will be fine. Even if everything isn't fine, it will all work out in the end. Don't panic.
"I don't think driving that motorised esky down the main street while you're pissed is very safe."
"Ah, no worries, mate. She'll be right."
Shirtfront: A shirtfront is a term taken from the game of Aussie Rules, and literally means; to run shoulder-first into an opponent's chest to knock him to the ground. Made unintentionally famous when a former Aussie prime minister threatened to shirtfront a Russian president.
Shit load or Shit ton: A unit of measurement. A very large amount.
Shonky: If something is shonky, it has been/is being done illegally. If someone is behaving in a shonky manner, they are behaving in an underhanded way and are performing underhanded dealings. Therefore a 'shonky setup' is a business that is engaged in criminal activity or is not being run in a legal manner.

Shed: A storage or containment building originally made of corrugated iron or tin, more recently made with 'Colorbond' metal sheeting. Sheds can range from small (a garden shed), medium (a standalone garage), large (a barn, stables or shearing shed) to very large (an aircraft hangar).

Sandgroper: A person from Western Australia. See Westie.

Sanger *(sang-uh)*: A sandwich.
Sausage sizzle: A lovely barbecued meal to be had on a weekend. The wonderful thing about sausage sizzles is they can pop up anywhere. They are also cheap.
Screamer *(scream-ah)*: A spectacular mark taken in the game of Australian Rules Football.
Screw: To fornicate. Not to be confused with Screw loose.
Screw loose: Someone who is eccentric.
"He's got a screw loose."
Servo: A fuel outlet where you can also get a hot pie, unless they're being slackers.

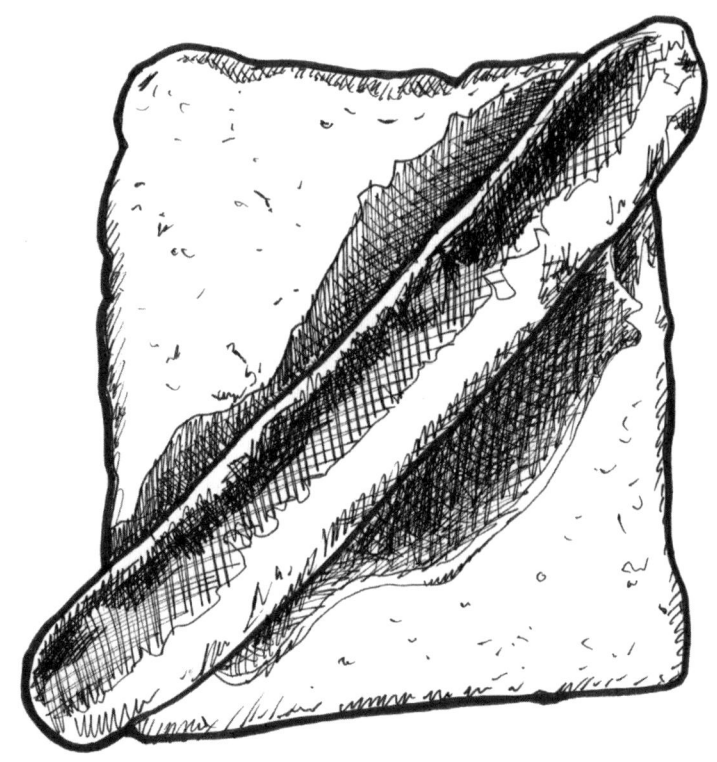

Root: Sexual relations. Never one to be subtle, the Aussie male may compare himself to a wombat; one who "eats, roots and leaves."
It is surprising there are any human Aussie offspring at all.

Rubber: Due to alternative meanings, the use of the word, "rubber" has been frowned upon in the Australian school system for a number of years. What it actually means is an eraser. Therefore, if someone is drawing or writing using a pencil, and asks you for a "rubber", they are not asking for a condom, they are requesting to borrow an eraser.

opinion." In the second instance it will be accompanied by a raised eyebrow or a disbelieving look that will confirm your suspicions.

Red Back: A venomous spider.

Ripper: Wonderful, great. "She's a ripper" can refer to a great looking girl, a car, a boat or an animal.
"It's a ripper of a day" is self-explanatory.

Roo: A large marsupial with strong back legs that jumps when it moves. Do not confront the male of the species. See Boomer.

Rack off: "I do not want your company, thank you. Please leave."

Ranga *(rang-uh):* A red-headed person.

Rashie: A type of shirt worn for (mostly) water sports.

Ratbag: Usually used as an affectionate term for someone who causes a bit of trouble, unless the ratbag in question is doing something truly criminal.

Reckon: A very common term in Australia. When someone is giving an opinion, it will usually end in, "I reckon", or "I don't reckon", which will show you what that opinion is. "Ya reckon", is merely a shortening of the question, "What do you reckon", though it can sometimes mean, "I don't agree with you, but you are entitled to your ridiculous

Q

prefers the night. Four distinct types; Western or Chuditch, Spotted-Tail, Eastern, and Northern. On the Endangered species list.

Quokka: a friendly furry marsupial native to Rottnest Island off the coast of Western Australia.

Quoll: *(Kwoll)*: A lively spotted little fellow with sharp teeth, the Quoll

Pub: A meeting place where one can have a few Bevvies, eat a Parmi, and watch the Footy.

4) **Taking the piss:** to tease mercilessly. A national Aussie pastime.

Piss and wind: When someone is "all piss and wind", or "full of piss and wind", they are talking a voluble amount of insincerity. They do not mean what they say, or what they do say cannot be regarded as fact.

Pissed as a Fart: A phrase to describe someone who is extremely inebriated.

Piss-tank: One who drinks a lot of alcohol.

Pollie: A politician.

Pom: "Prisoner of Her Majesty"; An Englishman. See Whinger. Many Aussies are of English descent. It does not prevent them from calling anyone with a British accent a "Pom". No offence is intended.

Prang: A minor car accident.

Prawn: Large shrimp. We do not "put another shrimp on the barbie". We do that with prawns.

Pearler *(per-lah)*: Wonderful, great. See also ripper.
Pig: A derogatory term for a policeman.
Pigroot: A term used of horses - when bucking with head down and hind legs kicking.

Pig's ring: Something that isn't going to happen.
"Hey mum, I reckon I'll go up the road to see me mate, Danny".
"Pig's ring you are, boy". Translation, "No, you're not."
Piss: Aside from the usual meaning, piss can be used to describe a number of different things.
1) Pissed, drunk. Naturally one drinks piss to get pissed. Some Americans have had problems in Australia when an Aussie has said, "Let's get pissed" as in America when one is pissed they are angry. Aussies have adopted this term in recent years, but they still get pissed when they're on the piss. Sometimes one can be both.
2) Pissed off: to be angry.
3) Pissing down: raining heavily.

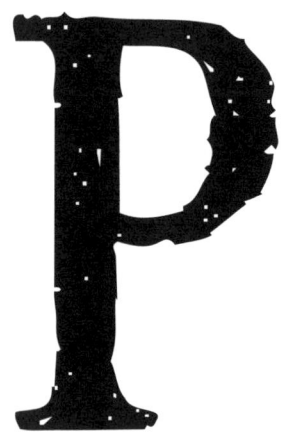

Parmi (or Chicken Parmi) *(par-mee)*: A popular counter meal at the Pub.

Pash: Making out or kissing for an extended period.
"Where's Terry?"
"He's out the back having a pash with Kylie."

Pav: Pavlova, a dessert consisting of a pie-shaped meringue covered with cream and fruit. Ongoing arguments exist between the Aussies and Kiwis as to who invented it. It's quite simple.
We did.

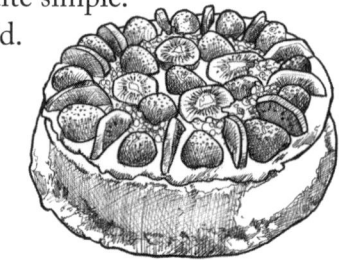

Station or farm country, desert or wilderness. Only Aussies know where the outback truly is.

Out back of beyond: See Outback.

Out woop-woop: see Out in the sticks.

Out in the sticks: Refers to an isolated rural area. "She lives out in the sticks." Also, can be used in a derogatory way for someone who does not live in the city area.

Ow are ya *(Ow-AHH-ya)***:** The distinction on this pronunciation is on the AHH, but it is said very quickly as one word. Means; "How are you?"

around the place and they're calling to each other. Keeping this in mind, when it is said three times and runs together to make the sound "oioioi", consider it a gentle warning.

Oldmate: A friend, lover, partner or pet. Can also be the older gentleman "down the road".

Op shop/Oppie: Opportunity shop, e.g. Good Sammies, or Vinnies. Where you can get yourself a bargain.

Outback: Refers to the Australian Interior. When one thinks of the outback it brings to mind visions of red dirt, snakes, lizards, brumbies, crocodiles and waterholes. In reality, the outback can be

Off his/her dial: To be severely affected by alcohol or drugs. In this instance "dial" means head.

Off like a bride's nightie: To leave.

Oi *(oy)***:** Said sharply as a warning, or shouted sharply to attract someone's attention (think of it as a word that always has an exclamation mark at the end it). When someone says or shouts "Oi", always check to make sure it's not you they're calling or warning. Oi may be a short word, but it means a lot. When it is shouted three times in quick succession, there are a bunch of Aussies

Numbat: The endangered 'Banded anteater' lives a solitary life in Eucalyptus woodland areas. Contrary to its other common name, it only eats termites. Ants are just an added extra.

Nurries:
1) A shortening of the phrase, "No worries".
2) The testicles.

"Mate, can you give us a hand? I bogged the ute next to the dam",
"No worries."
No worries has also been verbalised as, "No wukking furries" *(pronounced wuck-king fuh-rees)* and "No wukkas'. It means the same thing and any Aussies worth their salt will understand you.

Nuddy *(nuh-dee)*: Without clothing. The phrase you will hear is; "In the nuddy."

Nah yeah: Yes.
Nipper: A young surf lifesaver, or junior footy player.

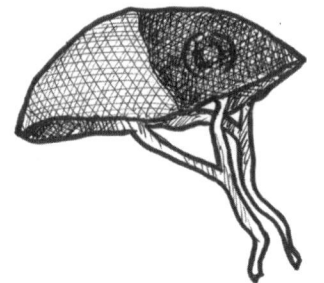

No worries: With similar verbal usage to the phrase "no problem", it is an acceptance and acknowledgement of what someone has said at face value. Some examples are as follows:
"Thank you",
"No worries."
"I apologise",
"No worries."

Munted: Broken.

Mexican: A term used for people who have crossed the border into a state above them, or who live in the state below. No walls or racism involved.

Mob:
1) A group of people.
"My mob" is my family or friends.
"That mob" is those people.
"Youse mob" is a group of people the speaker is talking to.
2) a group of sheep.

Mortein: An insect repellent especially useful for getting rid of flies, Red backs and Mossies.

Mossie *(moz-zie)*: A small biting insect that uses its proboscis to suck your blood. The best way to get rid of the little bastards is to whip out a can of Mortein.

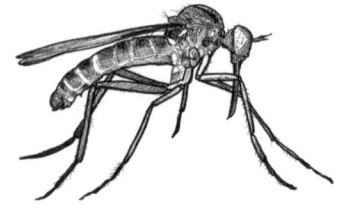

You can call someone you greet "Mate" if you do not know or remember their name.

It is not really the done thing for a male to call a female "Mate", though she can have mates, be one of your mates and call you mate. There are still many Aussie males who call females "mate" though. Don't be distressed, they are treating you as an equal.

You can also call someone "Mate" if you're not very happy with him "I'll have your guts for garters, mate," which roughly translates to, "I will make you wish you had never been born, my friend." It is obvious, when used in this way, that the person referred to as "mate" is not actually a friend nor one the speaker particularly likes.

When the word is extended to "Maaaaate", the speaker is either not impressed, or extremely impressed, by what someone has said or done.

Melbs: Melbourne *(pronounced Mel-bun)*, Capital City of Victoria

Mad as a cut snake: When you hear someone referring to another person using this term, it is best to avoid the person that is being described. When he/she is "as mad as cut snake", it can mean anything from, "completely insane with possible violent tendencies", to "crazed with fury." Accept it and move on.

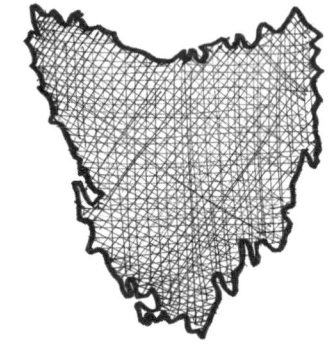

Map of Tasmania: Refers to the female genital region.

Mate: As with Bastard, "Mate" can have many meanings. You can have mates or be mates and you are all on friendly terms.

Laughing gear: Mouth. "Wrap your laughing gear 'round a burger"

Liddle bewdy: Little Beauty. Something that is very good.
Lippy: Lipstick.

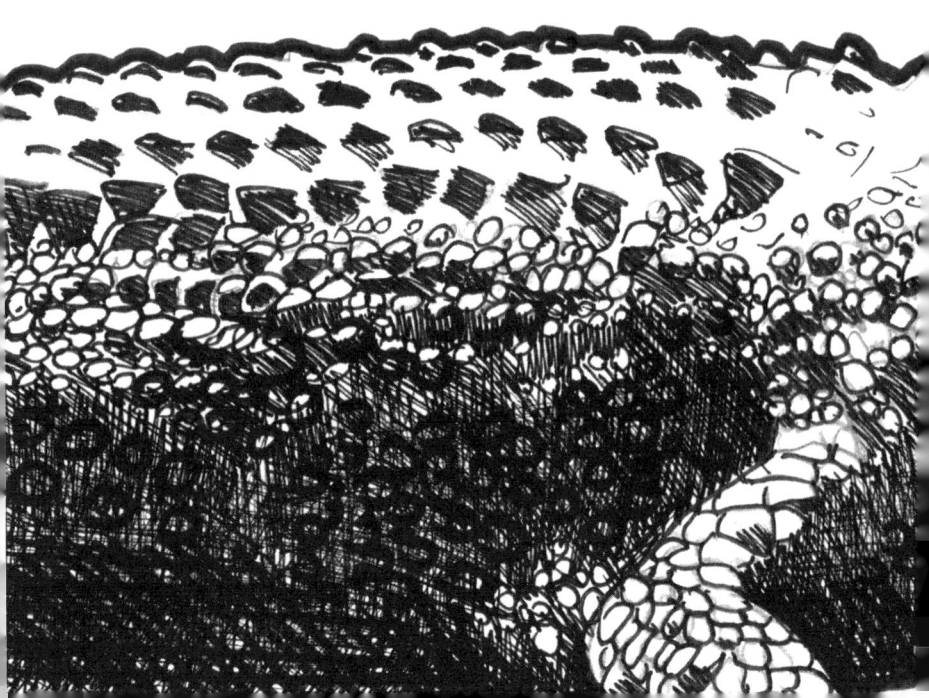

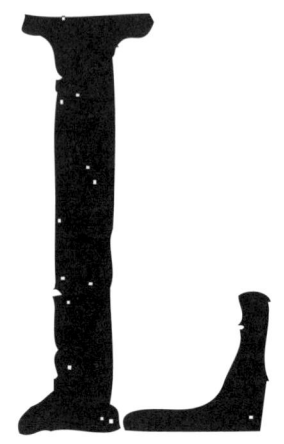

Lackey/ Lackey band: a lackey or lackey band is also known as a rubber band, or elastic band. Used on stationery, or in some instances as a hair lackey (an elastic band to tie back one's hair). When someone asks for a lackey they are not asking for a servant. From this, one can also assume when one is told to "use a lackey", one is not being told to get someone else to do it.

Lamington: A delicious finger food made from sponge cake coated in chocolate and rolled in coconut.

Lappy: Laptop computer. Therefore, if you hear someone say, "I'm on my lappy" or "I'm using my lappy", it does not mean they are being silly, it means they are using their laptop.

"Can I use/borrow your lappy?", is not a request to sit on your lap.

K

Kangaroo: See Roo, and Boomer.

Kindy: shortened from the word 'Kindergarten' it is an introduction to preschool before preschool. They do finger painting. It's fun.

Kiwi: A New Zealander

Koala: Sometimes incorrectly referred to as a koala "bear", this cuddly Aussie icon is not a bear at all; it is a marsupial or pouched mammal.

Kookaburra: A native bird sometimes called the laughing jackass.

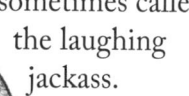

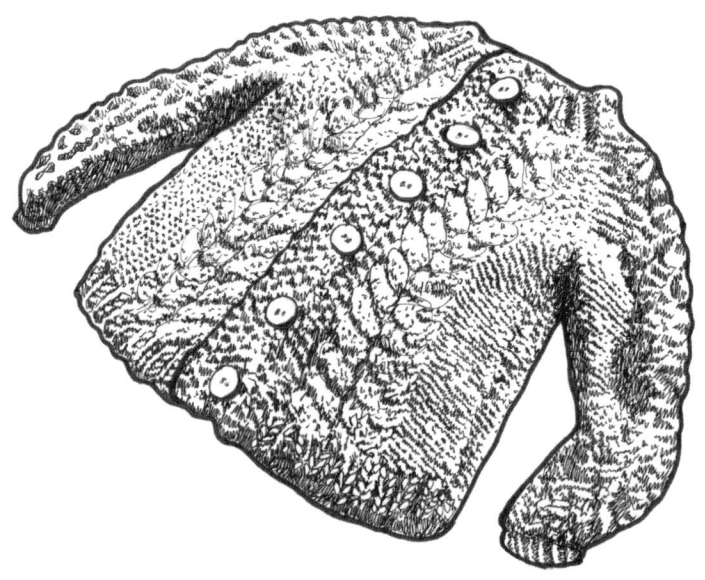

Joey: A pocket sized kangaroo. Also a shortening of the name Joseph.

Journo: One who works for the media in the role of story collecting and/or interviews.

Jumbuck: An old term for a male sheep or ram. This is not used in modern day language.

Jumper: A sweater, windcheater, pullover, or knitted… well… jumper.

J

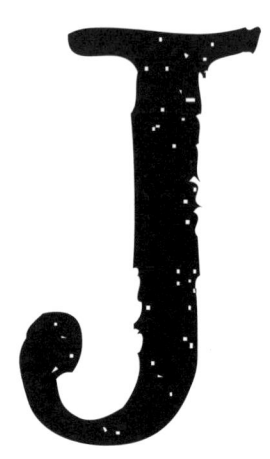

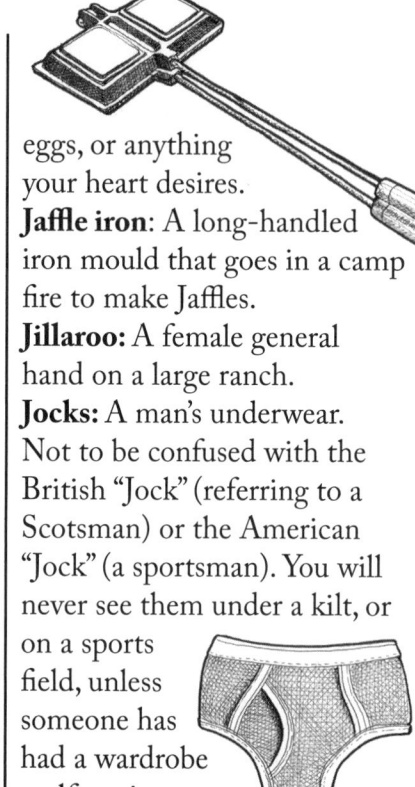

Jackeroo: A general hand on a large ranch (for "Ranch" see Station).

Jaffle: A toastie, or toasted sandwich made with a Jaffle iron. Can be filled with tinned spaghetti, baked beans, braised steak and onion, bacon and eggs, or anything your heart desires.

Jaffle iron: A long-handled iron mould that goes in a camp fire to make Jaffles.

Jillaroo: A female general hand on a large ranch.

Jocks: A man's underwear. Not to be confused with the British "Jock" (referring to a Scotsman) or the American "Jock" (a sportsman). You will never see them under a kilt, or on a sports field, unless someone has had a wardrobe malfunction.

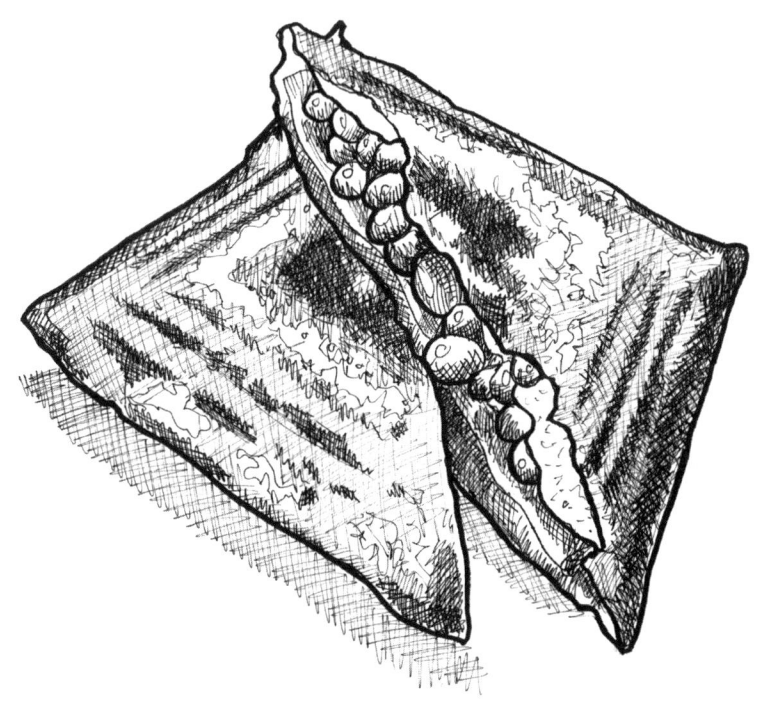

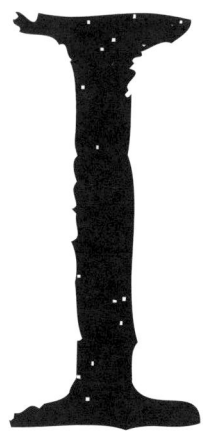

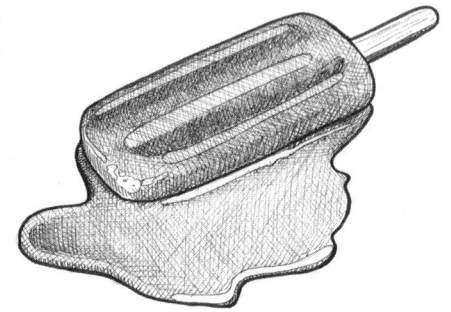

Ibis: The Australian White Ibis can now be found in suburbia and has acquired many nicknames, amongst them; "Bin Chicken" and "Tip Turkey". Though native, because of the increase in population the Ibis is now regarded as a pest in some states.

Icypole: An iced lolly, ice block or popsicle.

Hoon: Someone who drives too fast or recklessly. Hence the word "hooning". There is a law against hooning in Australia, so your best bet is not to do it, or your car will be impounded. This is not a joke.

Hooroo: A farewell.

Horse Doovers: A play on the french term: Hors d'oeuvre. Finger food to accompany alcoholic beverages; usually small red sausages on toothpicks.

Howsitgarn (how is it going): "How are you? How is life treating you? I hope you are well."

Howsithangin' (how is it hanging): See Howsitgarn. A satisfactory answer to this one would depend on which hand you use e.g. "to the left". The previous sentence is a joke.

Howyagarn (how are you going): See Howsitgarn. It is not a question as to how you are getting somewhere. The person asking is not concerned about your mode of transportation.

Hang about: "Could you wait a moment please?"

Happy little vegemite: Usually used in a sarcastic manner, this term would be referring to one's demeanour. When someone says. "Oh, you're a happy little vegemite aren't ya?" they are referring to your mood.

Have a go *(av-a-go)*: When you are "having a go" at someone, you are telling them off. When someone asks "You wanna avago?" it can mean they are asking you for a fight, or if you would like to try doing something new. But, "Old Avago" is someone who attempts to do things yet rarely gets them done properly.

Hogget: A half-grown sheep.

these things, or that someone has gone walkabout.
Going off like a two-bob watch: Complaining or arguing loudly. Can be shortened to simply "going off".

Goog (pronounced with *oo* as in book or cook): An egg, or googie egg

Goon: Cheap wine.
Gunna *(gun-ner)*: When someone is called, "a gunna", it usually means they have good intentions, but they're not going to complete whatever it is they are supposed to.

referred to as "Mate" unless they are ferals.

Geez *(jeez)*: Has the same meaning as gee whizz.

Gilgie *(jil-gee)*: A freshwater crustacean found in Western Australia. See also Yabby.

Give it a burl: Try it out.

Give it a crack: Give it a try.

Goanna:
1) A large lizard.
2) A music band.

Going bush:
1) To go camping in the bush.
2) To go to a remote area to work.

Note: when someone has gone bush, it can mean either of

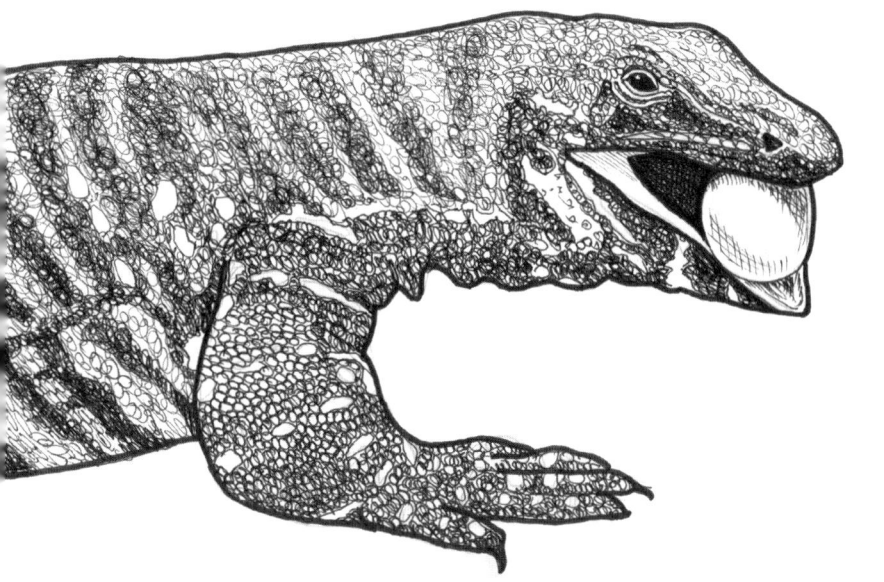

Galah *(gull-Lah)*:
1) a type of bird
2) an idiot, or person behaving in a ridiculous manner.
A "bunch of galahs", is a group of people behaving in a ridiculous manner.

Garn:
1) Go on e.g. "Garn, get him", "Garn then, I dare you."
2) Going e.g. "How's it garn"

Gasbag: to have a chat, or talk a lot.

Gawd:
1) An exclamation of disbelief or disgust.
2) A call to a religious entity.

Gawdluvim: "God love him". An affectionate term for one who has done something that may cause ridicule.

G'day *(gid-ay)*: Aussie greeting. May be used instead of "Hello". One can also say "G'day mate", but only to Aussie males. Most Aussie females would rather not be

Firey: A fireman.

Flat stick: To drive or run extremely quickly.

Fluff:
1) Fart.
2) A mistake
3) A mistress.

Please refer to the content of the conversation when using this word. You do not want to mix them up.

Footy: Australian Rules Football (not soccer).

Franger *(Frang-uh)*: Condom.

Frig/Friggin': A polite way of saying a much harsher word.

Frootloop/s:
1) A breakfast cereal.
2) A person whose mental faculties may be called into question. "Yeah, I'm not too sure about him, he's a bit of a frootloop."

Full as a goog: To have a full stomach, either from eating or drinking. Literally, "as full as an egg."

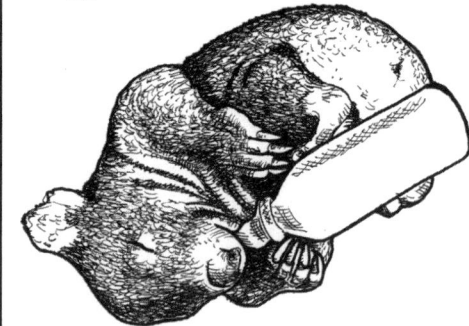

Furphy *(phurphy):* Something that isn't exactly true. A lie. "Nah, mate, that's a bit of a furphy."

Feral:
1) An animal or amphibian not native to Australia.
2) A description used for a person, place or thing that is wild or unkempt.

"That mob is a bunch of ferals", translates to, "The group of people we are discussing have no manners and are probably carriers of infectious disease."

"The place is feral", translates to, "The building is in disrepair, not very clean, and I wouldn't touch it with a ten-foot pole."

Fair go: Another term used in diverse ways. If you are having a go at someone and they reply with "Fair go", it means they are asking you to be gentle or fair. When you are asked to give someone a fair go, you are being asked to treat them fairly. This is one saying that can and will be extended to sentences like, "Fair crack of the whip, mate." or "Fair shake of the sauce bottle, mate." If you hear "fair" at the beginning of the sentence, you are more than likely being asked to give someone a fair go.

Fairy bread: A party food of candy sprinkles on bread to be eaten by small children.

Fan-bloody-tastic: Wonderful. Can also be used sarcastically;

"I'm sorry I dinged your car."
"So am I. Do you have insurance?"
"No, I don't."
"Fan-bloody-tastic."

Echidna *(ee-KID-nah)*: Also known as the Spiny Anteater, this cute, shy but prickly little mammal is one of the few who also lays eggs.

Emu: *(EE- mew)* : A large and ridiculous bird who cannot fly. No, he can't.

Esky: A portable cooler or icebox for storing cold food and drinks. Known as a "chilly-bin" in New Zealand.

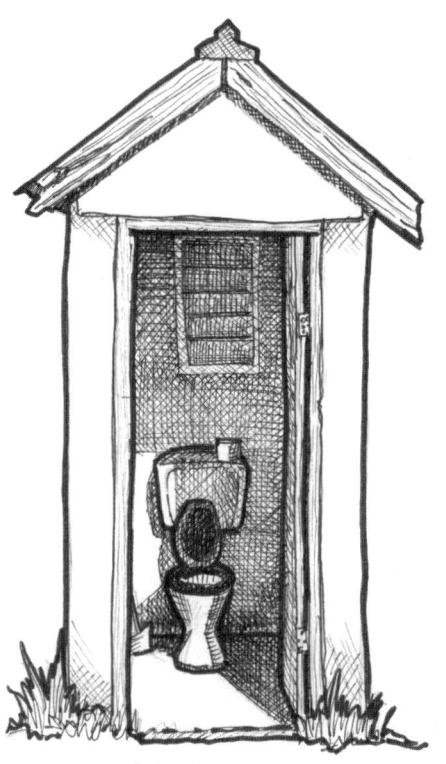

Drop Bear: An imaginary, terrifying marsupial that attacks from the treetops. Perhaps this phrase originated from a sleeping Koala that fell out of a tree.

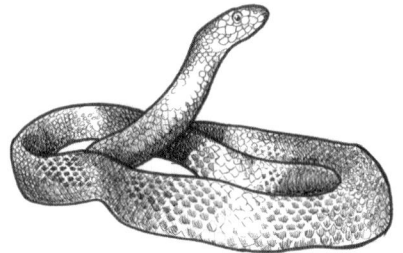

Dugite: An extremely angry, venomous and dangerous snake, native to Western Australia. Ranges in colour from, grey, green, yellow, brown and black. Large scales. Head is small and indistinct from body. Can grow up to 2 metres (6 feet 7 inches).
Dunny: A toilet.
Durry: A cigarette.

Dog Ugly: Unattractive. "I don't like the look of that bell tower. It's dog ugly."

Dole: A government payment to support a person who is unemployed.
Dole Bludger/Dolie: One who is currently receiving government handouts or the "dole".
Donga: Temporary or demountable housing.

Doona *(doo-nuh)***:** A duvet or quilt like covering for a bed.
Doughie/Doughnut *(doe-wee, donut)***:** A tight circular manoeuvre performed by a car or motorbike, usually accompanied by a lot of smoke and the occasional tyre catching fire.
Down the road: One would usually expect, when someone says "just down the road", the object or person may be only a few minutes away. This is not necessarily true. A place could be miles away, but because of the vastness of the Australian countryside, or it will be regarded as being "just down the road".

Defo *(deaf-oh)*: Definitely.
Devo *(Dev-oh)*: Devastated.
Digger: Commonly refers to a veteran soldier of World War 1 or 2, though it can refer to anyone, male or female, that has served in the Australian New Zealand Army Corps.
Ding: A dent, usually on a vehicle.
Dob: If you dob on someone, you are telling a person about someone else's wrong doing or "talking behind someone's back". Now, while informing on criminal activity, drug dealers etc could be considered dobbing, it is not because that activity is affecting the community in a negative way. If you are dobbing on someone for accidentally having their water on once at the wrong time of the day, for children playing loudly in the backyard next to yours, for someone not turning up to work that one time because they're hung over, then you are a dobber.
Dobber *(dobber-In)*: A "tattle-tale", a "grass"; someone who informs on other's misdemeanours for their own benefit. Australia's modern history is built on convicts and, with this history firmly in mind, Aussies do not appreciate a dobber.

used by modern Aussies when affectionately referring to someone who is slightly eccentric, is a bit of a character, or has done/said something silly. Therefore, when someone calls you a "bloody dag" they are not comparing you to dried poo hanging off a sheep, they're calling you a silly bugger in the nicest possible way.

Deadly/ Too deadly: Contrary to its usual meaning, this word does not necessarily refer to something life-threatening. It does, in fact, mean that something is fabulous or cool.

Deadly Treadley: A bicycle.

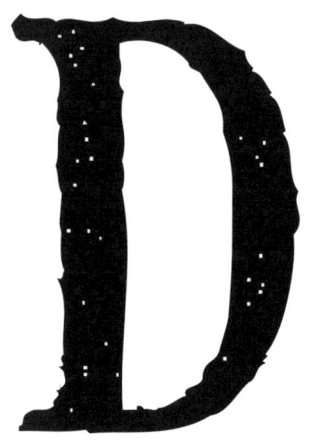

Dacks: Underwear, pants or trousers, depending on the occasion.
Most commonly heard as:
"Get your dacks on."
"I'm gonna get some new dacks."
"He dropped his dacks."
"Pull your dacks up."
"Let's dack him," meaning let us remove his pants. Strange, but true.

Dag: Originally used as a term meaning the dried dung hanging off a sheep's hindquarters, it is still used today when a cockie needs to "dag the sheep" (remove the stuff).

'Dag' is more commonly

as a salty, but you know they're better off left alone.

2) One of a pair of plastic shoes. If someone has lost a croc, or even a pair of crocs, it is no great loss. Offer to buy them a pair of thongs instead.

Crook: Although the word can refer to a thief or criminal, it also has the following meanings:

1) Feeling crook: to feel unwell
2) Going crook/went crook: Someone who is/was angry, and yelling about it.

Cuppa: A hot beverage. "I wouldn't mind a cuppa."

Cutting Up: To perform Doughies, squealies, and burnouts. "Cutting up the surface of the road."

Coonack/Koonac: A freshwater crustacean found in Western Australia. (See Yabby.) Not to be mistaken with Coonac, which is an historical mansion in Melbourne.
Cossie *(coz-zie)*: See Togs.
Cracker: Wonderful or terrific. "It's a cracker of a day." "What a cracker."
Crayfish: Unlike crawfish, the Southern Crayfish is a saltwater crustacean that is particularly delicious on a barbie. A clawless lobster. Also known as the Southern Rock Lobster.
Crikey: An exclamation one might make when excited, astounded or disbelieving. "Goodness me!"
Cripes: see Crikey
Croc: 1) A large amphibious reptile with many teeth. The last of the dinosaurs. Comes in two forms:
a) Salty; a salt water croc, the largest and most dangerous of the species.
b) Freshy; a fresh water croc. Not as large or as dangerous

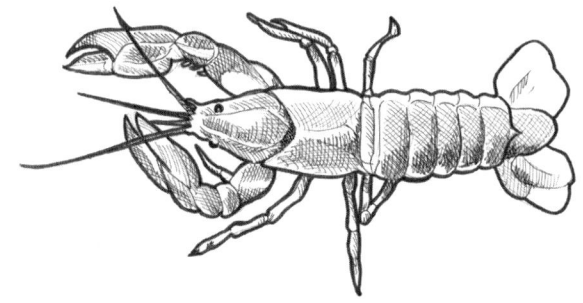

you're going the wrong way.
Circle work: See Doughie.
Clacker: Bottom or backside. "Fair up the clacker" means "right up the rear end."
Cob/Cobba: Another word for mate.
Cockie: A farmer

Cockles:
1) Shellfish found under mud or sand in saltwater areas.
2) A male's genitals. "He got one in the cockles" means he received a blow to his nether regions.

Cocky: A cockatoo. Pink and grey galahs are also called cockies, even though they're not.
Coldie: A beer.
Convo: Conversation.
Cool Drink: Soft drink, soda or pop. If you don't want a cool drink, but you would like a cold drink, then you should specifically ask for that.

Carton: A box of beer containing 24 cans. Also called a Slab or Block.
Chalkie: A school teacher.
Chateau de Cardboard: Boxed wine, or wine that comes in a cardboard carton.
Chewie/s: Chewing gum.
Chippie: A qualified carpenter (see Tradie)

Chockie *(chok-kee)*: a delicious food made from the cacao seed. Comes in dark, milk or white forms, and sometimes has fruit, nuts or candy added.
Chook: A chicken or hen. You can also go down to the supermarket for a cooked chook if you can't be bothered cooking tea.
Chrissy: Short for Christmas.
Chuck a sickie: What you do when you want a day off work.
Chuck a uey *(chuck-a-yewy)*: What you do in a vehicle if

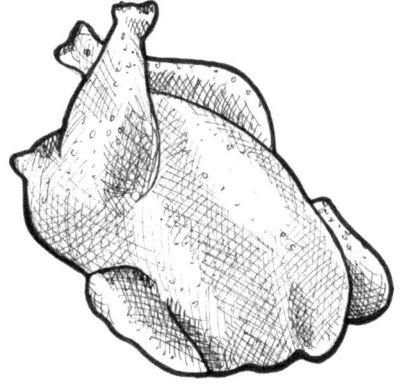

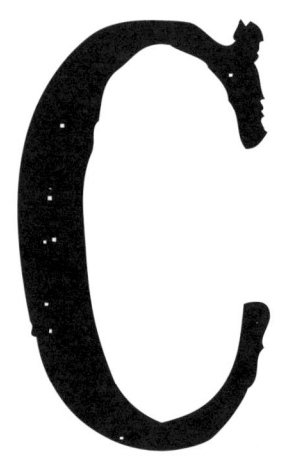

Cacking: Laughing a lot. To cackle.
"I was cacking myself." Means: I was laughing a lot.
Can also be used in the past tense.
"He cacked himself."

Cane toad: A football disguised as a feral amphibian.
Cardie: An item of clothing, a cardigan.
Cark it: To die.
"Gawd, mate, ya look like yer gonna cark it."
Carn: "Come on."
Carry on like a:
1) Blue-Arsed fly.
2) Pork Chop.
To get overly upset about not very much at all.

Bunnings: An international household hardware chain where you will usually find tradies wandering the aisles. Also, a great place to grab a sausage sizzle if you're feeling hungry.

Burnout: To make the wheels of one's car turn rapidly while the vehicle is stationary, which creates burning rubber, a lot of smoke, and the need for new tyres.

Bush/Bushland: Much of the Australian countryside is made up of bushland including low lying trees, wattle and eucalypts.

Bushie: One who prefers to live in the bush. A bushman (pronounced, 'bushmun').

Buzz box: A small car.

"Bugger off" "Please go away."
"Bugger this" (or "Bugger that.") Means
1) "I'm getting annoyed because the task I am trying to perform is proving difficult. I am about to stop doing it."
2) "I don't like the look of this/that."
"You little bugger." means "I'm not very happy with you right now." Note: this sentence can also can be said with grudging admiration.
"He's a big bugger." Means "He is very tall/large/long."
"Cheeky bugger." is self-explanatory.

"It's a bit of a bugger." Means it can to be difficult to do.
"Stop buggerising around!" Means "Please stop this foolishness." (Here, the word is pronounced, "*bug-guh-rise-ing*", but still as quickly as possible.)

Bum nuts: Chook eggs.

Bungarra *(bung-arra)*: A type of monitor lizard (very large), also known as the "racehorse goanna".

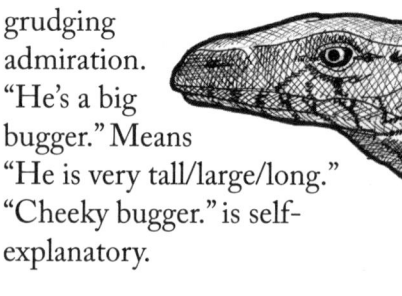

Buckleys/Buckleys and none: No chance. Therefore, if someone tells you, "You've got buckleys", they mean you don't have a chance in hell.

Budgie smugglers: Swimming briefs for men. Though usually reserved for athletes, budgie smugglers have been known to adorn the occasional prime minister and overweight middle-aged male.

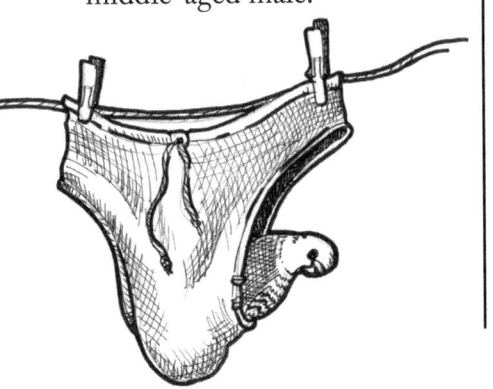

Bugger *(bug-guh)*: Yet another delightfully useful and interchangeable word, bugger can be used in a number of different scenarios. Please note, bugger is a word that is said quickly. It is not often one draws the syllables out, rather it spits out of the mouth as if one has inhaled a fly and is trying to get rid of it. Aussies do not consider "bugger" to be a swear word.

"Bugger." "Oh dear."

"Bugger me." "Well, I'll be damned!"

"Bugger it." Means
1) "It is frustrating and I'm giving up now."
2) "I'm going to do it anyway."

 **Booze Bus:** A specialised police vehicle that contains the instruments to do a random breath test. So, basically, where the cops take ya when you look a bit pissed and you've blown over on the handheld device. If you're really pissed, they'll whack ya in the traffic car or paddy wagon, and take ya back to the station. You'll be up the creek then.

Bottlo *(Bottle-oh)*: A liquor outlet.

Box:
1) A container of beer.
2) A television.

Brickie: A qualified bricklayer.

Brissie *(Brizzie)*: Brisbane (pronounced "Briz-bun"), Australia.

Broggie: A sliding stop or taking of a corner performed on a push-bike, motorcycle or vehicle, where the tail end and back tyre/s slide out sideways. This manoeuvre is performed on dirt or mud to make it specky. It is NOT quite the same as drifting.

Brumby: A wild horse or pony. Horses are not native to Australia.

Blue:
1) A fight or heated argument.
2) A nickname for a redheaded person.

Boardies: Board shorts. Most blokes would rather wear boardies than budgie smugglers.

Bog:
1) Spaghetti Bolognese.
2) Fecal matter.
3) To eat, "Two, four, six, eight. Bog in, don't wait."

Bogan *(boe-gun)***:** Similar in meaning to "Red Neck" in the America. Bogan usually has tattoos, wears uggies or thongs and is a bit rough around the edges.

Bonza: Great. An old Australian term, Bonza is not in use much in today's modern society.

Boomer: A male kangaroo. See also Roo.

Bloody hell *(blud-dy-ell)*:
1) "That gave me quite a fright."
2) "Would you look at that?" (disbelief)
3) "I can't believe I/you just did/said that."

Bludger *(Blud-jah)*: One who lives off government handouts and has no intention of working for a living. One can also be "bludging off" which means they are not doing their work to the best of their ability, or are having a slack day.

Bikkie: A biscuit to dunk in your Cuppa.

Billy: An old term for a pot or tin used over an open fire for boiling water. A more modern term for a kettle. "Put the billy on luv, and we'll have a cuppa."

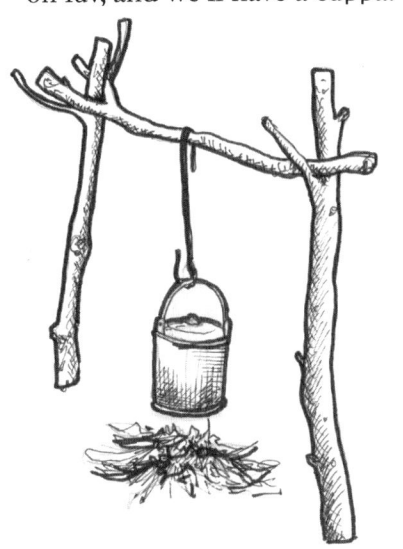

Bindi *(bin-dee)*: A prickle.

Bingle: A minor car accident or collision. "She had a bit of a bingle."

Blimey *(Bly-mee)*: Cockney in origin. See Crikey.

Bloody *(blud-dy)*: Does not often refer to something with blood on it. Bloody is a mild swear word that can be added in front of almost any other word. "You bloody idiot." "This bloody thing," "My bloody foot hurts." Or "My foot bloody hurts". Bloody can be used freely in conversation between friends. It is like an exclamation mark in the middle of a bloody sentence.

can mean the speaker is calling a friend an affectionate name. "You bastard!" can also mean that someone is not particularly happy with what someone has just done. "That bastard!" is taken the same way. It is a particularly good idea, when hearing the word "bastard", to look at the general demeanour of the person saying it. If they are smiling, it's okay. If they appear angry, then it's not. If they are neither smiling nor appear angry, it is probably a good idea to listen to the conversation in its entirety.

Bevvie: a beverage, usually alcoholic.

Bewdy, mate *(beauty mate)*: Thank you very much, I appreciate it.

Beyond the black stump: Very far away.

Barney: An argument.

Barrack/barracking: When you "barrack" or "are barracking", it's usually for someone, something, or a team of someones or somethings. Therefore, when you are asked, "Who are you barracking for?" the person is asking who you are cheering for. This term has a different meaning to the usual British definition of "loud shouting by someone who disagrees with a person who is speaking". It is loud shouting, yes, but it is for, not against.

Bastard *(baa-sted)*: Rather than referring to one being born out of wedlock (something that does not concern most Australians), Bastard can be used in a number of different ways, depending on inflection, the sentence the word is used in, or the general mood of the person saying it. "You bastard,"

Back of Burke: Far away.
Bad Trot: A run of bad luck.
Banana Bender: A person from Queensland. Also known as a Queenslander.

Barbie: A barbeque. A hot plate and, in recent times, outdoor oven. Also refers to an outdoor "get together" where snags, steaks and prawns are cooked. If invited around for a barbie see Carton, Chateau de Cardboard and Slab.

Ay: (as in hey but without the H) You will often find this strange expression at the end of a sentence which may make other words near it sound odd, or lead you to believe the speaker has a speech impediment. This is not the case. When someone says, "Ay", they are expecting you to agree with what they have just said. It will not usually be posed as a question with the telltale rising inflection at the end of the sentence, which may cause confusion.
"It's a nice day, ay". (The speaker is not a stutterer.)
"Yeah, it's pretty good, ay." (the speaker is not saying hello.)

keeping operations" and "the contribution and suffering of those who have served". Originally to honour those Anzac's who fought at Gallipoli against the Ottoman Empire during World War 1, it has since expanded to include all our brave fighting men and women. Aussies can get extremely offended by those who do not understand the importance of this day.

Arty-farty: Derogatory term. 1) A sensitive artist or person of uncertain sexuality. "Yeah, I don't really want to visit Joe Blow, he's a bit too arty-farty." 2) An object, room or building where the artistry is perhaps misunderstood. The speaker does not like it.

Arvo: The afternoon. "What are you up to this arvo?" "I'm gonna pop around to the olds in the arvo."

Avachat: One who talks a lot. "Did you see Mrs Murphy up the road this arvo?" "Oh, you mean old avachat?"

Aussie Rules: Australian rules football.

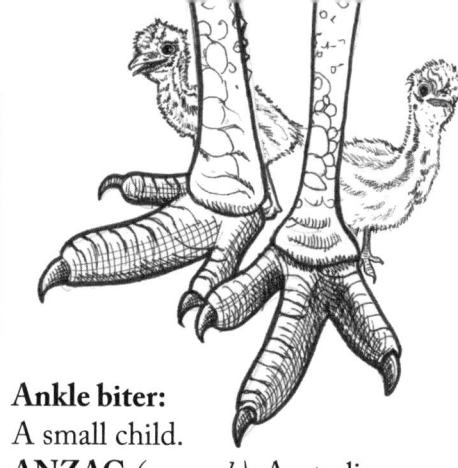

Agro *(agg-roe)*: Angry.
Amber fluid: Beer
Ambo *(am-boe)*:
A person, male or female, who drives or works out of an Ambulance.

Ankle biter:
A small child.
ANZAC *(an-zack)*: Australian New Zealand Army Corp or member of.
Anzac Day: A national day of remembrance on the 25th April in Australia and New Zealand to commemorate those who have served in the armed forces: "those who served and died in all wars, conflicts and peace-

The Top Secret Guide to
AUSTRALIAN
SLANG

Kate Capewell
Illustrations Marion Duke